Picturing Lincoln

Picturing Lincoln

Famous Photographs That Popularized the President

by GEORGE SULLIVAN

Clarion Books
New York

Clarion Books
a Houghton Mifflin Company imprint
215 Park Avenue South, New York, NY 10003
Copyright © 2000 by George Sullivan

The text was set in 13-point Goudy.

Book design by Michelle Gengaro-Kokmen.

For information about permission to reproduce selections from this book,
write to Permissions, Houghton Mifflin Company, 215 Park Avenue South,
New York, NY 10003.

www.houghtonmifflinbooks.com

Printed in the USA.

Library of Congress Cataloging-in-Publication Data

Sullivan, George, 1927–
Picturing Lincoln / by George Sullivan.
p.   cm.
Includes bibliographical references (p. 85) and index.
Summary: Examines some of the famous photographs taken of President Abraham Lincoln,
discussing the circumstances under which they were taken and how these images were used.
ISBN 0-395-91682-8
1. Lincoln, Abraham, 1809–1865—Portraits—Juvenile literature. 2. Presidents—
United States—Pictorial works—Juvenile literature. 3. Photography—United States—
History—19th century—Juvenile literature. [1. Lincoln, Abraham, 1809–1865—Portraits.
2. Presidents—Portraits. 3. Photography—History—19th century.] I. Title.

E457.6.S85   2000
973.7'092—dc21
[B]   00-027576

CRW 10 9 8 7 6 5 4 3 2 1

Contents

Acknowledgments

In selecting the images of Abraham Lincoln used in this book, I was fortunate to be able to draw upon the collections of photographs and prints of some of the nation's foremost historical and cultural institutions. Special thanks are due the curators, photo researchers, librarians, and archivists representing these collections. They include Mary Ison and Maja Keech, Prints and Photographs Division, Library of Congress; Cindy VanHorn, the Lincoln Museum at Ford's Theatre; Mary Panzer, Heather Egan, and Jodi Fain, the National Portrait Gallery; Zina Davis, Museum of American Political Life, University of Hartford; Sal Alberti and James Lowe, Alberti/Lowe Collection; Julie Simic, Lilly Library, University of Indiana; Eileen Kennedy, Museum of the City of New York; Cynthia Matthews, Chicago Historical Society; Patrick Keeffe, Cooper Union; Shannon Perich, National Museum of American History; Joann K. Lindstrom, Tioga County (New York) Historical Society; and Michael Maione, Ford's Theatre Museum.

Acknowledgments

Special thanks are also due Cecilia Wertheimer, Bureau of Engraving and Printing, U.S. Treasury Department; Jonathan Mann, publisher, *The Rail Splitter*; Skip Theberge, National Oceanic and Atmospheric Administration; Daile Kaplan, Swann Galleries; Martin Gengerke, R. M. Smythe & Co.; Edmund B. Sullivan; Lloyd Ostendorf; Ellen LiBretto; Chuck Myers; Steven Laschever; David Wong; and JoAnn Lewis of the *Washington Post*, for her article on October 12, 1997, suggesting "there's a Brady portrait in your pocket."

Picturing Lincoln

Reach into your pocket and you'll probably find a portrait of Abraham Lincoln—in the form of a penny. Or dip into your wallet, where you may have a five-dollar bill—another likeness of the sixteenth president.

The portraits of Abraham Lincoln that appear on the penny and the five-dollar bill are but two examples of the great outpouring of Lincoln images produced during his lifetime and in the years following his tragic death.

Printed portraits of the president and items featuring his image—including the penny and the five-dollar bill—had one thing in common. They were all based on photographs. Artists and engravers simply copied the portrait images of Lincoln that had previously been captured by photographers of the time. In Lincoln's day, copying photographs by hand was a highly developed art form.

According to Lloyd Ostendorf, who has studied Lincoln photographs for more than half a century, there were about 130 different original photographs taken of Abraham Lincoln. He was photographed on sixty-six different occasions by a total of thirty-six cameramen.[1]

Five of the 130 photographs were more widely copied and distributed than any of the others. They are: a portrait made in Chicago in 1857, when Lincoln was forty-eight years old, beardless, and not yet nationally known; a photograph made by Mathew Brady in New York City in 1860; and three photographs taken at Mathew Brady's Washington, D.C., studio early in 1864—the famous penny profile, the five-dollar-bill photo, and a portrait of Lincoln with his son Tad. These five original photographs and the many ways in which they were re-created and used are the subject of this book.

Photography, the technique of producing an image on film or other material, was invented in 1839. The earliest known photograph of Lincoln was made in 1846, in Springfield, Illinois, when Lincoln was thirty-seven. This portrait is a daguerreotype, a term that refers to an early photographic process in which a highly detailed picture was formed on a silver-coated copper plate.

In the daguerreotype process, no negative was produced. No prints could be made from it. Thus, the first photographic portrait of Lincoln was seen by only a small number of people. Even as late as 1860, when Lincoln was getting ready to run for president, relatively few people had any idea what he looked

This daguerreotype, which dates from 1846, is the earliest known photograph of Lincoln. It is owned by the Library of Congress and is often on exhibit there.
Library of Congress

like. The general public wanted to know. And once he had captured the nomination and officially entered the race for the presidency, the demand for likenesses of Lincoln grew stronger.

This demand was satisfied not only by photographs but also by engraved portraits, which were copied from photographs.

3

Such portraits were printed in magazines, newspapers, and books.

Lincoln's campaign to win the presidency required broadsides, or printed circulars, that featured his image. These were put up on fence posts or nailed to tree trunks. Banners and flags were also common. Lincoln's supporters wore buttons, badges, and ribbons that carried his portrait.

Later, during his White House years, engravers and printmakers continued to sell a multitude of printed portraits, many of which were meant for home display. Small card photographs, called *cartes de visite*, were mass-produced

This Lincoln photograph, possibly taken by C. D. Fredricks, dates from 1861. It later served as a model for a wood engraving by W. G. Jackman.
Author's collection

4

and distributed by the tens of thousands. Scores of books, pamphlets, and song sheets featured engravings of the president. Portraits of him were also painted.

Lincoln's death in 1865 stunned Americans. He was the first president to be assassinated. He had just led the country through a long and bloody war, and it was assumed that he would preside over a period of renewal. Memorial portraits of him flooded the marketplace. Mourning badges and ribbons, medals and tokens, most bearing the image of the martyred president, were put on sale. Publishers and printers reissued famous photographs of him, now edged in black.

In 1909 the one hundredth anniversary of his birth triggered the production of another great torrent of Lincoln memorabilia. The Lincoln penny dates to 1909. More printed portraits, tokens, and medals were turned out. Postage stamps were issued in his honor.

Unlike modern presidents, Lincoln was never pursued by news photographers. His White House staff did not include a photographer whose job it was to take pictures of him on a day-by-day, event-by-event basis, as is the case today.

The technology of photography in the 1860s made it difficult to record action-filled events. A cumbersome "wet plate" process was used in taking photographs. Because exposure times were many seconds in length, the slightest movement by the subject caused a blur. As a result, photographers worked mainly in studios, where they could control the lighting and other conditions.

There were exceptions, of course. There is a famous

photograph of Lincoln with General George B. McClellan and members of his staff at the Antietam battlefield near Sharpsburg, Maryland, in 1862. But this was not typical. Usually Lincoln visited a photographer's studio to have his picture taken.

Today, we buy film in rolls of twenty-four or thirty-six exposures. But in Lincoln's time, there was no "roll film." Instead, the image was exposed on a rectangular glass plate that had been coated with a sticky mixture of wet collodion. The finished print was the same size as the glass plate.

The glass plate was placed in the camera while still wet.

After the exposure was made, the plate was developed immediately. It was then washed and the image "fixed"— that is, made permanent.

In the 1860s the technology did not exist to enable newspapers or magazines to reproduce photographs as they do today. Instead, they used engravings made from photographs.

To make an engraving, an artist copied or traced a photograph onto a block of hard wood. The artist would then cut the image into the wood, a long and difficult process. Last, the block would be inked and prints made from it. (Later, metal was used instead of wood.)

Engraved images were also used to picture news events. James F. Gibson's photograph of a Civil War field hospital at Savage's Station, Virginia, taken in 1862, became the model for this woodcut version of the scene.
Library of Congress

The resulting wood engravings—or woodcuts, as they were called—were used as illustrations in *Harper's Weekly, Leslie's Illustrated Newspaper*, and other newspapers and magazines of the time. It was from these illustrations that millions of Americans got an idea of what the notables of the day looked like. Wood engravings were also created to depict important news events.

The "wet plate" process of photography was a big help to artists and engravers who made woodcuts for illustration purposes. It enabled photographs to be printed directly onto the woodblock from which the engraving was made. Engravers then had a perfect guide as they cut the image into the wood.

Lithography was another popular printing process of Lincoln's time. The process is based on the fact that water and grease do not mix.

In producing a lithograph, an artist draws the photograph in reverse on a special flat stone with a greasy crayon. To print the image, the stone is dampened with water and ink is applied. Then paper is pressed to the surface of the stone. The ink is absorbed by the paper wherever there are no crayon marks, and the print is created.

Lithography, which was invented in 1796, represented a step forward from simple woodcut illustrations. It allowed artists to be more creative. They could produce images with a greater array of tones and textures.

On several occasions, Lincoln visited Mathew Brady's studio on Pennsylvania Avenue near C Street in Washington, D.C., to have his picture taken. Almost a mile south and east of the White House, the four-story building (at the extreme right in the photograph) still stands, as does the turreted structure at the left.
George Sullivan

But it was not until the 1880s, when the halftone process of duplicating photographs came into wide use, that woodcuts and metal engravings began to fade in popularity.

Whether the final product was a woodcut or a lithograph, it was usually based on a photograph. And, in Lincoln's case, the photograph was most likely one of the five featured in this book.

These photographs and their printed copies were intended to give people an idea of what Lincoln looked like. Later, they had other goals. They were used to help cast Lincoln as a "man of the people," as Honest Abe, as a family man, and as the Great Emancipator. After his death, they were used to portray him as the "savior of the Union" and the nation's "noblest son." They provided images for the mind and eye that have lasted to this day.

Alexander Hesler's tousled-hair portrait of Lincoln, taken in Chicago on February 28, 1857. It is the second known photograph of Lincoln.

Library of Congress

Chapter 1

The Tousled-Hair Photograph

The first photograph of Abraham Lincoln to be copied by printmakers was taken in Chicago in 1857. Lincoln had just passed his forty-eighth birthday.

At the time, he was deeply involved in politics again after a period of about five years in which he had devoted himself to his law practice. He was now looked upon as one of the leading lawyers in Illinois.

What drew Lincoln back into politics was an abrupt change in the national attitude toward slavery. In 1854 Congress had passed the Kansas-Nebraska Act. This law permitted settlers in the Kansas and Nebraska territories to decide for themselves whether they wanted slavery.

Lincoln had always opposed slavery, although he had not campaigned for its abolition. He expected that it would die a natural death. But the Kansas-Nebraska Act paved the way for slavery's growth and expansion, and Lincoln was upset.

His distress caused him to reenter the political field. He helped organize the new Republican Party in Illinois. During the presidential campaign of 1856 he gave more than fifty speeches in support of the Republican candidate, John C. Frémont.

Meanwhile, Lincoln kept busy with his law career. Indeed, 1857 was the busiest and most profitable year of his professional life.[1] Early that year one of the lawsuits in which he was involved required him to travel to Chicago. He also planned to do some campaigning for the Republicans.

While he was there, some of his lawyer friends asked him for a photograph. Lincoln had none. But he agreed to have one taken, and on February 28, 1857, he visited Alexander Hesler's Photographic & Fine Art Gallery.

"I don't know why you boys want such a homely face," Lincoln said jokingly. "I'm really not dressed to have my picture taken."[2] The clothes that he happened to be wearing that day shouldn't have been his only concern. His hair presented a more serious problem. He would later comment that his "rough hair" was "in a particularly bad tousle at the time."[3]

Almost all of the portraits taken of Lincoln over the years show him with a full head of hair. Usually it was parted on the left side, though occasionally the part fell on the right. But in this portrait there is no part. Before taking the picture, Hesler brushed Lincoln's hair away from his forehead, and then Lincoln himself tried combing it with his fingers.

Lincoln looks comfortable and relaxed in the photograph, his mind at ease. But his rumpled mass of hair is the portrait's

chief feature. He later recalled that a newsboy was given a supply of the pictures to sell. "Here's your likeness of Old Abe!" the boy shouted to potential customers. "Will look a good deal better when he gets his hair combed!"[4]

In a letter to James F. Babcock, the editor of the *New Haven Palladium* and one of his most active political supporters, Lincoln said he considered Hesler's photograph to be "a very true one." But, he continued, his wife and many others disagreed with that opinion. "My impression," said Lincoln, "is that their objection arises from the disordered condition of my hair."[5]

Lincoln returned to Springfield and continued to busy himself with his law practice. He also kept active in politics, and in 1858 he was nominated by Illinois Republicans to run for the Senate seat held by Stephen Douglas, a Democrat. That summer and fall the two men held a series of public debates in several small towns in Illinois.

Slavery was the key issue of the day. Lincoln believed the country was headed for a crisis over slavery. "A house divided against itself cannot stand," he had said. "I believe the government cannot endure permanently half slave and half free."[6]

E. H. Brown's engraving was based on Hesler's photograph. It is the first print of Lincoln ever published. Brown's print, a lithograph, later became known as "the Wigwam print."
The Lincoln Museum

13

Frederick T. Stuart, a Boston-born painter and engraver who, at the age of twenty, opened a studio in Newton Centre, Massachusetts, created this wood engraving, notable for its close resemblance to the Hesler photograph.
Library of Congress

Although the election was close, Lincoln lost. But something good happened. As a result of the debates with Douglas, Lincoln's name became known in other parts of the country. He began to be mentioned as a possible candidate in the presidential election of 1860.

Lincoln didn't pay too much attention to such talk at first.
His plan was to run again for Douglas's Senate seat in 1864.
But when Republican leaders launched a Lincoln-for-president
campaign, he did nothing to stop them.

In mid-May 1860 the Republicans met in Chicago to
choose their presidential candidate. The convention site was a
huge, specially constructed building that was nicknamed the
Wigwam. Lincoln himself did not become involved in the
frantic events that were to take place at the convention. He
remained in Springfield, allowing his shrewd manager, David
Davis, to handle matters.

The candidate to beat for the nomination was William
Seward, a U.S. senator from New York and the leader of the
Republican Party. Yet many believed that Lincoln, although
not well known outside Illinois, could overcome Seward's
advantage. Lincoln's firm opposition to the expansion of
slavery appealed to many Republicans.

Davis sent out members of the Lincoln team to talk with
various state delegations, insisting that Seward didn't control
enough votes to win. And Davis arranged for thousands of
Illinois Republicans to travel to Chicago, assigning them to
demonstrate at the convention on behalf of Honest Abe.

Lincoln waited anxiously in Springfield for news of what
was happening. He was almost certain that he was not going
to win.

When Lincoln's name was placed in nomination on the
morning of May 18, thousands of his supporters in the
Wigwam's balconies filled the convention hall with loud

In 1860 Thomas Doney, who had been an engraver and printmaker for more than fifteen years, produced this engraving, another version of the Hesler photograph. Doney restyled Lincoln's hair, softening the rumpled locks in order to make the candidate look more appealing. He did this, at least in part, by darkening the photograph's background so that the wild strands of hair became effectively camouflaged.
Library of Congress

cheers, the roar all but lifting the roof. The clamor continued for several minutes.

The delegates who supported Lincoln had been given copies of a printed portrait of the candidate based on Hesler's photograph of 1857. The portrait was the work of E. H. Brown, a Chicago engraver.

The print had no caption, perhaps because those who had ordered it weren't quite certain how it was going to be used. For example, if it had been labeled "The People's Choice for President," it would have been useless had Lincoln become a candidate for vice president.

Lincoln's name appeared under the portrait, along with a

Throughout the presidential campaign of 1860, Lincoln was portrayed as a person of integrity. He was the rail-splitter, the candidate with whom ordinary Americans could easily identify. The song "Honest Old Abe" was meant to underscore his trustworthiness. Besides "Honest Old Abe," there were a dozen or so other Lincoln songs, everything from polkas to marches, written for the campaign. In creating the cover for the sheet music of "Honest Old Abe," the artist reversed Hesler's portrait—that is, presented it as a mirror image of the original portrait. This was sometimes done to make it appear as if the pose was a new one.

The Lincoln Museum

credit for Hesler's photograph. Below Lincoln's image were the words "State Sovereignty [and] National Union," the motto of the state of Illinois.

During the outpouring of enthusiasm for Lincoln, his backers released a great mass of the printed copies of Brown's engraving. The storm of prints fluttered downward, peppering the heads of delegates with Lincoln's image.

It is obvious that Marcus Waterman, an Italian-born painter who maintained a studio in New York City throughout the 1860s, modeled his portrait of Lincoln after the Hesler photograph. But instead of minimizing the state of Lincoln's rumpled hair, as other artists had done, Waterman exaggerated it, making it a leading feature of the portrait.
Library of Congress

The Tousled-Hair Photograph

When the balloting began, Seward showed his strength, getting the most votes on the first ballot. But he did not receive enough votes to win the nomination. Lincoln was not far behind. In subsequent rounds of balloting, delegates were allowed to cast their votes for a different candidate. On the third ballot the "wildly excited" convention nominated Lincoln. Lincoln's supporters in the balconies released another torrent of printed portraits. George William Curtis, the editor of *Harper's Weekly* and a delegate to the convention, was in the convention hall that day, and he captured one of the prints. It survives at the Lincoln Library in Fort Wayne, Indiana. On it, Curtis wrote in pencil: "These prints were showered through the Wigwam immediately following Lincoln's nomination May 1860."

In the days that followed the convention, copies of E. H. Brown's print were passed around throughout the city of Chicago. Most people agreed that it was a rather harsh example of what the candidate really looked like. It was called "crude." But it didn't matter how the print was described. It had served its purpose.

Alexander Hesler took Lincoln's photograph again a few weeks after the convention, on June 3, 1860. The results were much more satisfying. Of Hesler's second photograph, Lincoln said, "[It] looks like and expresses me better than any I have seen."[7] This time, it must be noted, Lincoln's hair was neatly combed.

The Cooper Union photograph of Lincoln, taken at the New York studio of Mathew Brady, has been described as "the photograph that made Lincoln president."
Library of Congress

Chapter 2

At Cooper Union

After Lincoln was nominated as the Republican Party's presidential candidate in May 1860, he faced a serious problem. Few people outside Illinois knew much about him. He was a mystery candidate.

What little easterners knew of him suggested that he was a hardworking member of the Republican Party in the West. He was known as being opposed to slavery but willing to "leave slavery alone" in those states where it already existed.

Voters wanted to know, however, where he stood on other issues of the day. They were also curious about him as a person. What was his background? What did he look like?

Lincoln's supporters in the East were deeply concerned. How could their candidate be expected to attract voters if he remained so little known?

21

When it came to publicizing Lincoln, those who managed his campaign in the East wanted no part of what they called the "awful pictures" of him that had been taken in Illinois. The tousled-hair photograph, in their opinion, made him look foolish. So they turned instead to a photograph that had been taken earlier in the year when Lincoln visited New York City and spoke at the Great Hall of Cooper Union.

Cooper Union had been founded in 1859 by the manufacturer and philanthropist Peter Cooper. Its purpose was to provide the working classes of New York with a wide range of educational experiences, and it offered courses in science, chemistry, electricity, engineering, and art. Its facilities included a library, museums, meeting rooms, and the Great Hall, one of the largest auditoriums in the United States. (Today, Cooper Union schools its students in architecture, engineering, and fine arts. As in the 1860s, tuition is free for all students.)

Lincoln had arrived in New York City on February 25, 1860. The next day, a Sunday, he attended Henry Ward Beecher's Plymouth Church in Brooklyn.

On Monday morning, February 27, the day that he was to speak at Cooper Union, members of the Young Men's Central Republican Union met him at the Astor House, where he was staying. They planned to take him on a sightseeing tour of the city. Hiram Barney, one of the members of the group, suggested to Lincoln that they stop at Mathew Brady's studio so he could have his picture taken. That sounded like a good idea to Lincoln.

At Cooper Union

To steady Lincoln's head during the sitting, Brady used a metal clamp known as an immobilizer.
Lloyd Ostendorf

23

The thirty-seven-year-old Brady, the foremost American photographer of the nineteenth century, was at the height of his fame. He and his camera "operators" photographed the most celebrated figures of the day, from presidents and their cabinet members to prominent men and women in the arts and sciences. (When the Civil War broke out in 1861, Brady organized teams of photographers to cover it. Brady's pictures now provide a rich visual history of the time.)

Brady was with the noted historian George Bancroft when Lincoln and his Republican escorts arrived that morning. Bancroft introduced Lincoln to Brady. While Lincoln chatted with Bancroft, Brady began to make preparations for the portrait.

Brady decided that he would take a standing picture of Lincoln, posing him beside a small table, his body facing slightly to the left, his left hand resting on a pair of books on top of the table. Lincoln wore a new suit that he had purchased in Springfield, a vest, and a white shirt with a black tie.

In making pictures in those days, a relatively long exposure time was necessary. The slightest movement resulted in a blurred image. Portrait photographers thus had to use an immobilizer, or head clamp, to hold the subject's head perfectly still.

Many thousands of copies of Brady's Cooper Union photograph of Abraham Lincoln were distributed as *cartes de visite*.
Author's collection

24

At Cooper Union

(Left) This head-and-shoulders version of Lincoln's Cooper Union portrait was made available in France as a *carte de visite,* thanks to the noted French photographer Eugène Disdéri. (It was Disdéri who in 1854 first produced photographs in the *carte de visite* format.) But a retouch artist softened Lincoln's features, styled his hair, and removed a mole near his nose. The result was a more kindly looking Lincoln. After the card appeared in the United States, it came to be known as "the French face of Lincoln."
Author's collection

(Right) John Chester Buttre, who began as a portrait painter and became one of the most noted printmakers and engravers of the nineteenth century, created this head-and-shoulders portrait of Lincoln, basing his engraving on Brady's Cooper Union photograph and duly crediting the photographer.
Alberti/Lowe Collection

Engravers didn't always copy photographs exactly. They sometimes made changes that conveyed their own feelings about a subject. An engraver in Leipzig, Germany, produced this version of the Cooper Union portrait, giving Lincoln a more somber, even gloomy, appearance. The engraver also reversed, or flopped, the image.
Library of Congress

In Lincoln's case, the head clamp, even when its support rod was extended to its full length, did not quite reach his head. The base of the stand had to be placed on a small stool.

There was another problem. "I had great trouble," Brady said later, "in making a natural picture."

He asked Lincoln whether he could "arrange" Lincoln's loose collar, and then began to tug it higher.

"Ah," said Lincoln, "I see you want to shorten my neck."

"That's just it," Brady replied, and both men laughed.[1]

The incident seemed to relax Lincoln. He stared calmly into the lens as his image was registered on the camera's

HON. ABRAM LINCOLN, OF ILLINOIS, REPUBLICAN CANDIDATE FOR PRESIDENT.

[PHOTOGRAPHED BY BRADY.]

When Lincoln became the Republican presidential nominee on May 18, 1860, *Harper's Weekly* was quick to react. In its issue of May 26, the magazine presented this engraving, which was derived from the Cooper Union photograph, giving credit to Mathew Brady as the photographer but not mentioning the name of the engraver. This may well be the first instance where the image of a candidate for high office appeared in a publication that represented what later would be called the mass media. In the engraving's caption and in the text of the short biography that surrounded the engraving, Lincoln's first name was misspelled— evidence, perhaps, that he was still not well known to easterners.

Author's collection

A. Lincoln.
HON. ABRAHAM LINCOLN.
SIXTEENTH PRESIDENT OF THE UNITED STATES.
Published by Currier & Ives, 152 Nassau St. N.Y.

This print, which was produced by Currier & Ives from Brady's Cooper Union photograph, was poster size, 14 inches by 18¾ inches, and was produced in color as a lithograph. It included an exact copy of Lincoln's signature, which was meant to increase its appeal. Mathew Brady was credited as providing the photograph that served as the print's model.

National Portrait Gallery, Smithsonian Institution

big glass plate. The result was an attractive, confident, statesman-like pose.

Brady had the negative retouched in order to correct a feature of Lincoln's left eye, which seemed to rove upward. The retouch artist also did away with some of the harsh lines in Lincoln's face.[2]

That night, in the midst of a fierce snowstorm, an audience of fifteen hundred turned out to listen to "the Westerner." Introduced by the editor and poet William Cullen Bryant, Lincoln began haltingly, reading from his manuscript in a high-pitched voice. But his confidence quickly grew, and he continued to speak for ninety minutes. The audience applauded frequently.

It was not a radical or revolutionary address. It was meant to reconcile the nation's sectional differences. Slavery was evil, Lincoln told the audience. The majority of the Founding Fathers saw it as such. Its extension to the territories was wrong, he said. "Let us have faith that right makes might, and in that faith, let us, to the end, dare to do our duty as we understand it."[3]

When he ended, the huge crowd stood and cheered, and some waved hats or handkerchiefs. Lincoln was surprised and pleased by the enthusiastic response.

The next day four New York newspapers printed the full text of the speech. The *New York Post* praised Lincoln for "using his rare powers solely and effectively to elucidate and convince [and] to delight and electrify as well."

Lincoln left the following day by train on a trip to New

England and a reunion with his son Robert, who was attending Phillips Exeter Academy in New Hampshire. During the two-week trip Lincoln delivered speeches almost every day. By the time he returned to New York it was obvious that his eastern tour had been a great success. Many were now convinced that he must be given serious consideration as a presidential candidate.

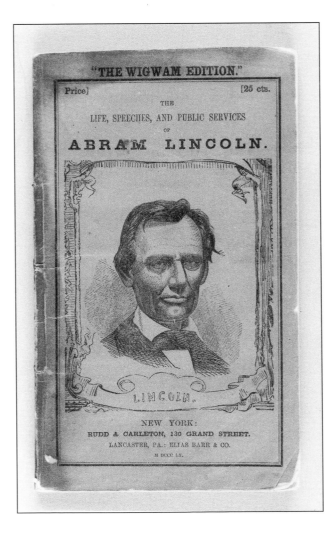

During 1860, twenty-two campaign biographies of Lincoln were published. "The Wigwam Edition," written by an unknown author and published by Rudd & Carleton, a New York firm, was one of them. Getting the biography into the hands of the public as quickly as possible was vital. Lincoln was nominated on May 18. Less than three weeks later, "The Wigwam Edition" had been printed and was ready for distribution.

Museum of American Political Life/Steven Laschever

At Cooper Union

* * *

Once Lincoln won the nomination in May, the photograph that had been taken by Brady in February acquired enormous importance. Prints of it were supplied to the major weeklies, *Harper's Weekly* and *Leslie's Illustrated Newspaper*. Both published versions of the photograph were made from wood engravings.

Brady's Cooper Union photograph was the first Lincoln portrait to draw the attention of eastern printmakers. Even Currier & Ives, the nation's foremost publisher of prints, was interested in it. Hesler's tousled-hair picture had never appealed to them.

Lincoln and his Republican backers also benefited from "cardamania." The term referred to the public's craving to acquire *cartes de visite*, which measured 2¼ inches by 4¼ inches and which bore the likenesses of the notables of the day. Card photographs were unknown in the United States when Lincoln had posed for Hesler in 1857. But three years later the Cooper Union *cartes* of Lincoln were sold to an eager public by the thousands.

The Cooper Union image was also lithographed for display in homes and offices. It was copied onto campaign broadsides, buttons, and badges. It was used as a cover portrait for biographies of Lincoln.

Silas Hawley, an agent for a crayon portrait of Lincoln, wrote to a friend in 1860 that "the country is flooded with the pictures of Lincoln, in all conceivable shapes and sizes, and cheap. The newspapers have his likeness; it is in medal form;

HONEST ABE TAKING THEM ON THE HALF SHELL.

In this political cartoon, titled "Political Oyster House," which was published in 1860, an artist altered Lincoln's Cooper Union portrait to give the Republican candidate a wide grin. And instead of a high collar and tie, Lincoln now wears a loose-fitting shirt that is open at the neck.

In election politics of the 1860s, Republicans spoke of Democrats as being either "hard shell" or "soft shell." Hard-shell Democrats were strongly in favor of slavery, while those classified as soft shell took a more moderate stance.

Here, Lincoln pauses to decide which of two "oysters"—that is, soft-shell Stephen A. Douglas or hard-shell John C. Breckinridge—to devour. Lincoln says, "These fellows have been planted so long in Washington that they are as fat as Butter. I hardly know which one to swallow first."

Museum of American Political Life/Steven Laschever

it is on envelopes; it is on badges; it is on cards; it is, indeed, on everything, and everywhere. And all for a *few cents*."[4]

Lincoln's chances that fall were boosted when the Democratic Party broke into two factions, the Northern Democrats and the Southern Democrats. A fourth party, the Constitutional Union Party, also put forward a candidate. In the election Lincoln received less than forty percent of the popular vote. But in the Electoral College he was the clear-cut winner, gaining more electoral votes than his three opponents combined.

Although the Cooper Union photograph played a role in Lincoln's election victory, how much of a role is difficult to say.

Mathew Brady thought it was decisive. Francis Carpenter, a painter, once remarked, "My friend Brady, the photographer, insisted that his photograph of Mr. Lincoln, taken the morning of the day he made his Cooper Institute speech in New York... was the means of his election."[5]

Thousands of pins, buttons, and badges bearing the Cooper Union likeness of Lincoln were distributed during the campaign of 1860. In this example, Lincoln's image has been reproduced on a small metal disk, which was then mounted inside a metal frame. The reverse side depicts Hannibal Hamlin, Lincoln's vice presidential running mate. Often combined with patriotic ribbons, the pins and badges were worn to show one's support for a particular candidate.
Museum of American Political Life/ Steven Laschever

33

The Brady image was printed on silk and satin ribbons that were worn by Lincoln supporters. The ribbons were also used as bookmarks.

Political ribbons had been introduced a decade or so earlier. These examples, one of which includes the portrait of Hannibal Hamlin, exhibit a "clarity of detail unrivaled by . . . any previous political ribbons," according to Edmund B. Sullivan, author of *American Political Ribbons and Ribbon Badges.*

Museum of American Political Life/Steven Laschever

Brady had some reason for so believing. On Sunday, February 24, 1861, not long before he was to be inaugurated, Lincoln arrived at a second studio that Mathew Brady operated in Washington, D.C., to pose for his first official photograph as president. Lincoln was escorted by two men, Allan Pinkerton, the noted Chicago detective, and Ward Hill Lamon, a lawyer from Springfield and a close friend, recently named city marshal of Washington, D.C.

George H. Story, a young artist who had a studio in the same building, was also on hand. Brady had asked Story to assist in posing the president-elect. Story later recalled that Lincoln

ABRAHAM LINCOLN.
Republican candidate for
Sixteenth President of the United States.

The E. B. and E. C. Kellogg lithograph company produced this elegant hand-colored print in 1860, which was greatly influenced by Brady's Cooper Union photograph. The artist, however, presented Lincoln in a seated position and added a background that included a stately column and rich drapery with graceful folds.
National Portrait Gallery, Smithsonian Institution

An unknown artist carved Lincoln's Cooper Union portrait into a piece of whale ivory to create this unique campaign memento. "Wide Awake" was a motto identified with a great number of spirited Young Republicans who clamored for Lincoln's election.
Museum of American Political Life/Steven Laschever

did not utter a word. He "seemed absolutely indifferent to all that was going on about him; and he gave the impression that he was a man overwhelmed with anxiety and fatigue and care."[6]

Scottish-born Alexander Gardner, who managed Brady's studio at the time and whose career would later rival Brady's, took five photographs during the session. Brady must have been hovering in the background. When the session ended, Lamon, who apparently did not realize that Brady and Lincoln had previously met, said to the president-elect, "I have not introduced Mr. Brady."

Engravers, lithographers, medal designers, and portrait painters weren't the only ones to turn to the Cooper Union portrait when creating Lincoln images. So did sculptors. This small bust of the beardless Lincoln was made of parianware, an unglazed form of porcelain that was popular from the late 1840s through the 1880s. Inscribed with the words "Constitutional Freedom," the piece was produced for the election of 1860.

Collection of Edmund B. Sullivan

As Brady came forward, Lincoln extended his hand and said, "Brady and the Cooper Union speech made me President."[7]

It is safe to say that Lincoln was exaggerating. There were many reasons for his election victory. His Republican colleagues had supported him with great enthusiasm, with bonfires and demonstrations, rallies and parades. Hundreds upon hundreds of speeches had been delivered on his behalf. Even William Seward and Salmon Chase, who had been his

In its first issue following Lincoln's victory, *Harper's Weekly* featured the president-elect's picture on its cover in a clever adaptation of the Cooper Union portrait. The Brady photograph was first copied by an artist, who reversed the picture. The finished drawing was then pasted onto a fancy background, creating what might be viewed as a White House reception room. And this time *Harper's* spelled Abraham correctly.
Library of Congress

ABRAHAM LINCOLN.
SIXTEENTH PRESIDENT OF THE UNITED STATES.

In November 1860, some time after he had been elected president, Lincoln began growing a beard. The news that he had acquired chin whiskers took the printmaking industry by surprise. Overnight, all photographs, engravings, lithographs, and other prints that portrayed a clean-shaven Lincoln were out of date.

Almost immediately, artists and engravers began to produce prints that depicted a newly bearded Lincoln. But only a handful of people had actually seen his beard (or photographs of it). Artists and printmakers could only guess what it looked like, and their guesses often missed the mark. In the Currier & Ives version, shown here, an artist drew a beard onto the Cooper Union print of Lincoln. Although the artist depicted Lincoln as fully bearded, he was unable to show the true character of Lincoln's beard, which was trimmed at the sides and bushy at the chin.
National Portrait Gallery, Smithsonian Institution

closest rivals for the nomination, had been diligent in lending aid. And there was the party split that divided the Democratic vote.

Yet Lincoln surely realized the importance of the Cooper Union photograph, which showed the tall prairie lawyer from Illinois, whose face was unknown to the general public, as a man of intelligence, sincerity, and dignity, a presidential candidate with great appeal.

Modern technology enables us to store photographs in digital form, view them on a television monitor, and re-create them as prints. This makes it easy for photographers to tinker with images, to manipulate, adjust, and change them. But there's nothing new about such trickery. Photographers and printmakers of the 1860s did much the same thing.

In this sequence, the artist began with an engraving of Henry Clay (photo 1), a Kentucky senator and noted nineteenth-century statesman. The picture was reversed, and the head of John C. Frémont, an American explorer and the Republican candidate for president in 1856, was placed on Clay's body (photo 2). There were other alterations: Frémont's hand is on his hip, whereas Clay's hand was at his side, and a handsome chair has been added to the scene.

In still another version of the print (photo 3), Lincoln's head from the Cooper Union photograph replaces the head of Frémont. A small lamp has taken the place of the globe. This image was very popular as a card photograph throughout Lincoln's lifetime. When Lincoln grew a beard (photo 4), engraver John Chester Buttre simply added a beard to the existing print.

Photos 1–3: Library of Congress; Photo 4: National Portrait Gallery, Smithsonian Institution

Anthony Berger's profile photo of Lincoln, one of seven poses taken at Brady's studio on the afternoon of February 9, 1864.
Library of Congress

Chapter 3

The Penny Profile

On February 9, 1864, a bright and chilly day in the nation's capital, President Lincoln, in the company of portrait artist Francis B. Carpenter, paid a visit to Mathew Brady's studio on Pennsylvania Avenue for a picture-taking session. Both before his election and after it, Lincoln had posed for many different photographers. Dozens of pictures resulted. But the photographs that were taken at Brady's that winter afternoon are among the most notable ever made of him. Most people, in fact, when they think of Lincoln, think of him in terms of one of these portraits.

The president, along with Mrs. Lincoln and Carpenter, who had been granted permission to spend six months at the White House while working on a portrait of Lincoln, intended to take a carriage to Brady's studio, which was less than a mile away. They waited and waited, but the carriage did not arrive. In his account of the incident, Carpenter

43

quoted Lincoln as saying, "Well, we will not wait any longer for the carriage; it won't hurt you and me to walk down."[1]

The early morning had been cold, with temperatures dropping below the freezing mark, but the afternoon sun warmed the day. Even so, Mrs. Lincoln decided not to make the journey. The Lincolns' son Tad joined his father and Carpenter at Brady's later.

As the president and Carpenter were about to leave the White House, a family of visitors approached them and asked whether they might shake the president's hand. Lincoln agreed, reaching down to the little boys in the group. "The Lord is with you, Mr. President," said the boys' father, who then added, "and the people are, too, sir; and the people, too."[2]

Lincoln was surely cheered by these words of encouragement. These were difficult days for him. On April 12, 1861, about five weeks after he had taken office, the Civil War had erupted. It had dragged on and on. Now it was about to enter its fourth year, and his frustration was growing.

Since the Union victory at Gettysburg the previous summer, the two opposing armies had skirmished as if they were in a chess match, with neither side gaining much of an advantage, although there had been Union victories at Lookout Mountain and Knoxville. Still, the war's end did not appear in sight.

Because of battlefield casualties and desertions, and the fact that there were few new volunteers, the strength of the Union army was ebbing. On February 1, 1864, Lincoln had ordered a draft of five hundred thousand more men. "The war is eating

The Penny Profile

London-born painter, engraver, and teacher John Sartain, who arrived in Philadelphia in 1830 at the age of twenty-two, did much to popularize the use of pictorial illustrations in American magazines and newspapers. Examples of his work appeared regularly in *Sartain's Union Magazine of Literature and Art*, which he founded in 1849. This is Sartain's signed engraving based on Berger's profile photograph of Lincoln.

The Lincoln Museum

my life out," Lincoln said to his friend Owen Lovejoy. "I have a strong impression that I shall not live to see the end."[3]

Yet Lincoln had no thought of abandoning the task at hand. During 1863, when he had been asked whether he planned to run for a second term, he had often been vague in answering, being careful not to reveal his true thoughts. No president since Andrew Jackson had served more than four years in office, and there was a general feeling that the tradition of a one-term presidency should be continued.

But by early 1864, it was no secret that Lincoln would be

45

seeking reelection. A victory at the polls in November would indicate support for his war policies and be seen as an endorsement of his Emancipation Proclamation, which had taken effect on January 1, 1863. The proclamation freed all slaves in those parts of the nation still in rebellion.

While Lincoln did not broadcast his plans to seek a second term, he did begin maneuvering to capture the

Working from Berger's photograph, artist William Willard produced this striking portrait of the sixteenth president. Born in Sturbridge, Massachusetts, in 1819, Willard spent most of his career in Boston. *National Portrait Gallery, Smithsonian Institution*

46

Republican nomination. Whenever party leaders visited Washington, he made it a point to invite them to the White House to discuss election strategy.

His campaign for reelection may have been on his mind when he made the appointment to visit Brady's studio. Lincoln could recall how important the Cooper Union photograph had been in the 1860 campaign. It would be wise to have an arsenal of new photographs on hand for the forthcoming election struggle.

For the photo session, the president, who was to celebrate his fifty-fifth birthday a few days later, wore polished boots, an elegant black broadcloth suit with wide lapels, a white shirt, and a black bow tie. He had on a heavy gold watch chain that was looped through a buttonhole of his vest.

Anthony Berger, the thirty-two-year-old cameraman from Frankfort, Missouri, who managed Brady's studio at the time, is believed to have taken the photographs that day. There were seven different poses. They included not only the likenesses of Lincoln that appear on the penny and on a five-dollar bill but also a portrait of Lincoln and Tad.

Berger's profile photograph is the best known of all Lincoln profiles. Like the Cooper Union photograph, it was copied and recopied by artists, engravers, and other photographers. Several examples of the reproductions appear in this chapter.

This medal with Lincoln's profile was produced for the presidential election of 1864, when Lincoln opposed General George B. McClellan. With its patriotic ribbon in red, white, and blue, it was meant to be worn on a jacket or shirt, like a political button of the present day.
Museum of American Political Life/Steven Laschever

Victor D. Brenner, a talented designer of medals, was responsible for using the profile photograph as the model for

the Lincoln cent. Born in Lithuania in 1871, Brenner was ten years old when his father began teaching him the art of engraving. By the time he was thirteen, he was an apprentice in his father's workshop, where he carved brooches, other types of jewelry, and the letters and symbols used in creating stamps and seals.

Brenner later immigrated to the United States with a brother and a sister. He opened a studio in New York in 1906 and set to work designing medals and plaques.

In 1908 Brenner was chosen to create a commemorative plaque and centennial medal in honor of the hundredth

Victor D. Brenner's centennial medal honoring Lincoln. Lincoln's likeness on the medal is almost the same as that on the penny.
Library of Congress

48

When the Lincoln penny was first produced in 1909, Victor D. Brenner's initials appeared on the reverse side, at the bottom. After protests, they were removed. The initials were restored in 1917 and placed on the front of the penny on Lincoln's shoulder, just above the coin's rim.
U.S. Treasury Department

anniversary of Lincoln's birth, which was to be celebrated in 1909. For his likeness of Lincoln, Brenner relied on Berger's profile photograph.

Brenner was later asked to design the Lincoln penny. For this, he adapted the image that he had designed for the centennial plaque. In fact, the two are almost identical.

On the front of the cent, Brenner included the words "In God We Trust." Theodore Roosevelt, who was president at the time, didn't approve. He felt the use of that motto on a coin was in poor taste. But before the dies to be used in stamping out the coin could be completed, he had left office. His successor, William Howard Taft, backed the use of the motto.

Brenner's design for the reverse side of the coin was simple and tasteful. It included the words "One Cent," which were enclosed between the tops of two stems of durum wheat. Above were the words "E Pluribus Unum," Latin for "Out of many, one," the motto of the United States.

Great excitement greeted the introduction of the new cent,

Lincoln's portrait on the penny is almost identical to his likeness as it appeared on this memorial plaque, designed by Brenner in 1907.
Daniel E. Pearson

which was the first American coin to bear a president's image. People stood in long lines outside the Federal Reserve Bank in San Francisco to buy it. In New York, throngs milled about the Subtreasury Building in lower Manhattan, where the new penny could also be purchased.

The coin was not universally popular, however, and drew more than a few complaints. Some people said that a man of Lincoln's importance deserved to be commemorated by a coin of greater status than the lowly penny. But those who applauded the new coin said that since Lincoln was the people's president, the penny was most appropriate.

Other critics didn't like the idea of doing away with the

The Penny Profile

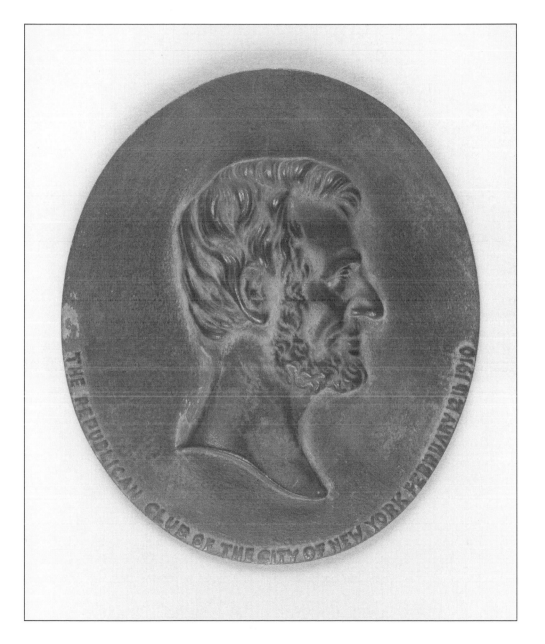

The penny profile has often been used on commemorative coins, medals, tablets, and plaques.
The Republican Club of the City of New York produced this example in 1910.
Museum of American Political Life/Steven Laschever

Indian-head penny, which had been in circulation since 1859 and was one of the most famous of all U.S. coins.

The loudest protests had to do with the placement of Brenner's initials—V. D. B.—on the reverse side of the coin. The letters were too big, it was said, too obvious. So intense was the outcry that the secretary of the treasury ordered that Brenner's initials be removed from the coin. But before the order could take effect, close to twenty-eight million V. D. B. pennies

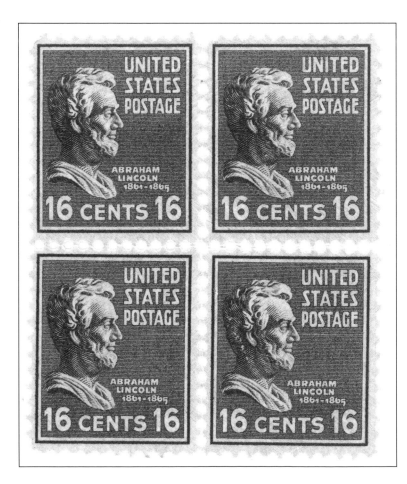

An engraving based on Berger's profile photograph of Lincoln was used not only on a coin but on a U.S. postage stamp as well. This sixteen-cent stamp, issued in 1938, was part of a presidential series.
Author's collection

had been minted. Today, these coins are highly prized by collectors.

In 1918 Brenner's initials were restored to the penny. This time they were stamped on the face of the coin, below the bottom of Lincoln's shoulder and just above the coin's edge. They are still there, but in type so tiny that the three letters can be read only by viewing a freshly minted coin with a strong magnifying glass.

In 1959 a new design that featured the Lincoln Memorial was introduced for the coin's reverse side. On the front the lettering has been restyled a number of times, but the Lincoln portrait has remained unchanged through the decades.

Many billions of pennies are minted each year. The General Accounting Office estimates that there are roughly 170 billion in existence. Berger's profile photograph of Lincoln surely ranks as the most reproduced work of art in history.

For the picture-taking session with his father at Brady's studio on February 9, 1864, Tad wore a dark suit and a tie. He also wore the same type of chain as his father wore. The Brady studio provided a photograph album for use as a prop. In the years that followed, as the photograph was copied and recopied, the photograph album was sometimes retouched to make it look more like a Bible, and occasionally it was even identified as one.

Library of Congress

Chapter 4

Lincoln and Tad

Abraham and Mary Todd Lincoln were parents of four children, all boys. Tragically, only one lived to become an adult.

Robert, the Lincolns' firstborn, arrived in 1843. Bobbie, as he was called, went to private school in Springfield as a young boy. He later attended Phillips Exeter Academy in New Hampshire and, after that, Harvard University. Lincoln seldom saw his young son during his boyhood years, and the two were not close.

The Lincolns' second child, Edward, born in 1846, never enjoyed good health. He died in 1850 from tuberculosis. William, called Willie, the third son, was born on December 21, 1850, ten months after Eddie's death.

When their fourth boy arrived on April 4, 1853, the Lincolns named him Thomas, after Lincoln's father. But because the boy had a large head, Lincoln called him his "little tadpole," then shortened it to Taddie or Tad.

Tad was born with a cleft palate, a defect in which the two sides of the roof of the mouth fail to join before birth. As a result, he sometimes garbled his words and spoke with a lisp. This probably caused Lincoln to draw closer to the boy and lavish him with affection.

Tad was Lincoln's pet. He could not say no to the boy. Tad did just about whatever he wanted to do and was often a "bad boy"—demanding, loud, and rude. That didn't bother his parents. Mrs. Lincoln called him "my little sunshine." But

Published by John Smith of Philadelphia, this is one of an array of prints produced during the 1860s based upon the photograph of Lincoln and Tad. The artist who created the print gave Tad a dressier appearance and added a decorative background.
The Lincoln Museum

Lincoln and Tad

LINCOLN FAMILY.

Photographers and printmakers of the time seized on the picture of Lincoln and Tad, using it as the centerpiece to create countless different parlor scenes that were offered to the public, sometimes as full-size prints, sometimes as card photographs. Pictures of other family members were often combined with the original photograph. In this version, Mrs. Lincoln has been added.

Author's collection

In this 1865 engraving, created by Adam Walter after Lincoln was assassinated, the family group has been expanded to include Robert Lincoln as well as his mother. Robert, who served on the staff of General Ulysses S. Grant during the final months of the Civil War, wears his captain's uniform.

To make for an appealing composition, Walter reversed the image of Lincoln and Tad. As a result, Tad is now at his father's right side (and the right-handed Lincoln is shown turning the album pages with his left hand).

To complete the family scene, Walter included a portrait of Willie Lincoln as a framed picture on the wall. Willie had died in 1862 at the age of eleven.

Lincoln Museum at Ford's Theatre

Lincoln and Tad

White House staff members and visitors realized that Tad was
just plain spoiled.

The special treatment that Tad received was reflected in the
fact that while Lincoln had his photograph taken well over a
hundred times, he never posed with his wife or any other
family member—that is, except young Tad.

The most famous picture of Lincoln and Tad, and the one
featured in this chapter, was taken on February 9, 1864, during
the session with photographer Anthony Berger at Mathew
Brady's studio in Washington, D.C. Lincoln is seated in Brady's

To capitalize on the popularity of Adam
Walter's engraving of the Lincoln family, the
New York publishers Moore and Annin
offered their own version of the scene.
Mrs. Lincoln and Robert look much as they
did in the Walter print, but Lincoln and Tad
have been restored to the places they had
in the Brady photograph.
Library of Congress

This engraving by John Chester Buttre was based on a black-and-white oil painting by Francis Carpenter. Carpenter had been present at Brady's studio on February 9, 1864, when Lincoln and Tad posed for Anthony Berger. In fact, Carpenter is said to have helped Lincoln and his son pose in an interesting manner, and he may have been the one who suggested using the photograph album as a prop.

Carpenter used the picture in his painting titled *The Lincoln Family* in 1861, which included not only Mrs. Lincoln and Robert but Willie as well. He painted the picture in black and white to make it easier for Buttre to produce his engraving. Carpenter later finished the painting by adding color.

Library of Congress

posing chair, holding a photograph album in his lap. Tad stands at his left and looks down at the album as his father turns the pages. Lincoln wore his eyeglasses for the picture, which he rarely did when being photographed.

Tad and his older brother Willie were the first presidential children to live in the White House. Lincoln was determined to "let the boys have a good time"—and they did. They gathered a multitude of pets, including ponies, rabbits, kittens, a turkey, a dog named Jip, and a goat, which slept in Tad's bed. Their play was often inspired by the Civil War, which raged during their White House years. They staged battles on the White House lawn, marched through White House corridors beating on toy drums, and, equipped with telescopes, set up a

This quiet parlor scene, published by Reilly & Sons, a New York and Philadelphia printmaker, must have been confusing to many people. Tad is made to stand in for his older brother Willie, while Tad himself is represented by the young child at the right, clinging to his mother's skirt.
Library of Congress

lookout station on the White House roof and scanned the grounds for "Rebs."

Tad was full of mischief. He broke mirrors, sprayed visitors with the White House fire hose, and dipped into the greenhouse fish tank to terrorize its occupants. He would stand in front of the staircase leading to his father's office and collect a five-cent "entrance fee" from those on the way to see the president, and he once locked his father in a little fenced-in park on Pennsylvania Avenue across from the White House. Presented with a box of tools, Tad drove nails into the antique mahogany desk used by Lincoln's secretary, John Hay.

"What will he do next?" White House staff members asked one another.

Tad and Willie had no formal schooling during the years they lived in the White House. Instead, Mrs. Lincoln hired a tutor for them. But Tad was so undisciplined that he could not or would not be taught. At eight he still could not dress himself. At nine he could barely read and write. Lincoln did not seem concerned, believing that Tad would become properly educated in time.

Willie was different. Gentle and intelligent, he understood that life was more than play. He was studious and loved to read. He kept a scrapbook, pasting in stories of important news events. Like his father, Willie had an exceptional memory. He even enjoyed learning train schedules by heart.

During church services Willie would sit and listen attentively to the preacher. Tad played on the floor with his jackknife.

Early in February 1862 Willie became sick. It is believed

Lincoln and Tad

Library of Congress

On Saturday, May 6, 1865, *Harper's Weekly* published a special edition, a memorial tribute to President Lincoln, who had been assassinated three weeks earlier. It included full-page engravings representing the scene at Lincoln's deathbed, the funeral procession in Washington, D.C., and the viewing of the body at New York's City Hall. On the front page, as a remembrance of the fallen president, was a full-page engraving of the Lincoln and Tad photograph.

A credit line beneath the engraving reads: "Photographed by Brady." Anthony Berger's name went unmentioned. It was not unusual in those days for a studio owner to be given credit for work actually performed by others. Besides, Berger's name was practically unknown to Americans; Brady's name, on the other hand, was a household word.

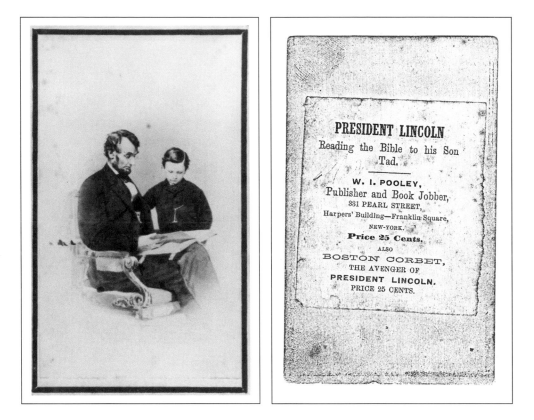

Edged in black, this card photograph was published to honor the memory of the deceased president. The caption on the reverse side of the card erroneously identifies the open volume that Tad and his father are looking at as the Bible.
Author's collection

that he may have had typhoid fever, a disease brought on by the polluted White House water system. The illness kept getting worse. Willie's temperature climbed, and he grew weaker and weaker.

Then Tad came down with a fever, too. A doctor assured the Lincolns that the boys would recover. Tad did improve, but Willie's fever raged out of control. He died on the afternoon of February 20, 1862.

Both parents suffered deeply. Funeral services were held in the East Room of the White House, but Mrs. Lincoln was in such a state of shock that she could not attend.

Lincoln grew even closer to Tad after Willie's death. He took him everywhere and would leave his office door open for the boy, who, late at night, often fell asleep on the office sofa as the president worked at his desk.

The photograph that was taken on February 9, 1864, was not the only one in which Tad and his father were pictured together. Almost exactly a year later, on February 5, 1865, Lincoln posed with Tad a second time. This photograph was taken by Alexander Gardner at Gardner's Washington, D.C., studio. Ten weeks later, Lincoln was assassinated.

In the years after his father's death, Tad often served as a teenage companion for his mother. "Only my darling Taddie prevents me from taking my life,"[1] she once wrote.

Eighteen-year-old Tad and his mother returned to the United States in 1871 following a long stay in Germany. They settled in Chicago. Soon after their return, Tad developed tuberculosis. The infectious disease took his life on July 15, 1871.

Mary Todd Lincoln, who had now experienced the death of three of her four sons and her husband's assassination, took refuge in spiritualism, believing that she could make contact with her dead husband. She lived alone in France for several years but eventually moved back to Springfield to live with her sister Elizabeth. Mrs. Lincoln died on July 15, 1882, the eleventh anniversary of Tad's death.

Lincoln and Tad

On February 5, 1865, Lincoln and Tad posed together a second time. Alexander Gardner, like Mathew Brady a premier photographer of the time, and once an employee of Brady's, was behind the camera. The photograph was taken at Gardner's studio in Washington, D.C.

This portrait of Lincoln and Tad was one of five photographs taken by Gardner that day. The others are formal poses, and they are among the most powerful of all Lincoln photographs, stunning portraits of the nation's war-weary leader. They were also the last posed photographs of the president. Ten weeks after the sitting, Lincoln was shot to death.
Library of Congress

Anthony Berger's imposing portrait of Lincoln, from which the famous five-dollar-bill engraving was made.

National Portrait Gallery, Smithsonian Institution

Chapter 5

The Five-Dollar-Bill Portrait

The dignified portrait of the seated Lincoln featured in this chapter is the image of the sixteenth president that is most familiar to Americans. Another of the photographs taken by Anthony Berger at Mathew Brady's studio on the afternoon of February 9, 1864, it is the portrait that is engraved on the original five-dollar bill. In fact, until the Treasury Department introduced a redesigned five-dollar bill in 2000, the picture was often called *the* five-dollar-bill portrait.

Robert Lincoln, the Lincolns' oldest son, considered it to be the best photograph ever taken of his father. Thirty years after his father's death, Robert wrote to Frederick Hill Meserve, who had assembled an enormous collection of Lincoln photographs and was considered the foremost authority on the subject: "I have always thought the Brady photograph of my father, of which I attach a copy, to be the most satisfying likeness of him."[1]

(Top) The first five-dollar notes to display Burt's engraving date from 1914. These were "large-size notes," measuring 3⅛ inches by 7⅜ inches.

(Middle) In 1923 the bill's design was changed, and the portrait of Lincoln became circular instead of oval. This is known as the "porthole" portrait of Lincoln.

(Bottom) In a series of notes first issued in 1928, the Lincoln portrait was oval again. These are the smaller-size five-dollar bills (2⅝ inches by 6⅛ inches) that were issued until the introduction of the newly designed five-dollar bill in 2000.

R. M. Smythe & Co./Martin Gengerke

The Five-Dollar-Bill Portrait

The engraving of the first of Berger's photographs used on the five-dollar bill was the work of Charles Burt, who was born in Scotland in 1822 or 1823. After immigrating to the United States and becoming a highly skilled engraver, Burt worked for a number of American banknote companies. He was under contract to the U.S. Treasury Department's Bureau of

The redesigned five-dollar bill, introduced in 2000, is based on another portrait taken by Anthony Berger at Mathew Brady's Washington studio on February 9, 1864.
Bureau of Engraving and Printing, U.S. Treasury Department

Engraving and Printing, which was established in 1864, when he created the now-famous Lincoln engraving.

It is only in fairly recent times that the image has come to be associated with the five-dollar bill. It was first used on other types of notes produced by the Bureau of Engraving and Printing. For example, it appeared on a series of one-hundred-dollar bills issued in 1869. These were slightly bigger than the bills of the present day.

As with other photographs of Lincoln, the earlier five-dollar-bill portrait was published as a card photograph. In this version the image was reversed and presented in its familiar oval form.
Museum of American Political Life/Steven Laschever

The cabinet card, a larger and more splendid version of the card photograph, was introduced in 1866. Measuring approximately 4½ inches by 6 inches, the cabinet card soon replaced card photographs in the public's favor, and it remained popular well into the 1880s. This is Mathew Brady's cabinet-card version of the five-dollar-bill photograph.
Alberti/Lowe Collection

A. Lincoln

ABRAHAM LINCOLN.

PRESIDENT OF THE UNITED STATES.

John Chester Buttre of New York engraved and published this print, based on Berger's earlier five-dollar-bill portrait, in 1864, the same year the photograph was taken. It was reproduced in a variety of sizes. William Momberger created the drawings that bordered Lincoln's portrait. These represent the western migration by Americans, the freedom granted slaves by the Emancipation Proclamation, the war to preserve the Union, and the era of peace that was expected to follow.

Ellen LiBretto Collection

In the election of 1864 Lincoln, the Republican candidate, faced Democrat George B. McClellan, the former commander of the Union armies. Those who backed the president could wear this stylish campaign pin.
Museum of American Political Life/Steven Laschever

Besides its use on the five-dollar bill, on other paper currency, and on an assortment of postage stamps, the photograph was also widely used as a mourning portrait.

When Lincoln was shot by John Wilkes Booth at Ford's Theatre on April 14, 1865, roughly five months after his election victory and just days after the surrender of General

The Five-Dollar-Bill Portrait

Charles Burt's engraving of the Berger photograph of Lincoln has also appeared on a great number of stamps, envelopes, and other philatelic items. Here are two examples: a five-cent stamp from an 1890–93 series and a three-cent stamp from a 1922–25 series.
Author's collection

One-hundred-dollar bills, measuring 3⅛ inches by 7⅜ inches were known as "large-size notes."
R. M. Smythe & Co./Martin Gengerke

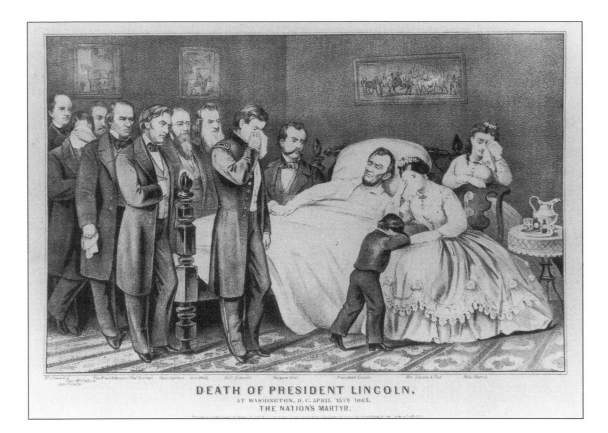

DEATH OF PRESIDENT LINCOLN,
AT WASHINGTON, D. C. APRIL 15TH 1865.
THE NATION'S MARTYR.

After John Wilkes Booth shot the president in Ford's Theatre on the night of April 14, 1865, Lincoln's mortally wounded body was carried across Tenth Street, up the stairs of a boarding house, and into a small bedroom. There the unconscious president was laid on a low walnut-frame bed. Throughout the night, as his life ebbed away, dozens of people moved in and out of the room. Many artists later sought to re-create the tragic scene. In this version, by Currier & Ives, the president's head from Berger's portrait has been grafted onto an anonymous body. This drawing, and others, included people who were not there. Young Tad Lincoln, for instance, shown here sobbing into his mother's lap, actually remained at the White House the night his father was assassinated.

Museum of American Political Life/Steven Laschever

Robert E. Lee, it sent shock waves through the nation. An enormous outpouring of grief followed. Printmakers were overwhelmed by orders for memorial portraits of Lincoln, which were then hung in homes, shops, and houses of worship. In addition, prints depicting the Lincoln family were wanted for home display. Mourning ribbons and badges bearing the president's image were also in great demand.

In New York City, Fox's Bowery Theatre hung a large

Napoleon I, emperor of France from 1804 to 1814, is believed to be the first to have posed in this fashion, slipping his right hand into his jacket. During the Civil War, Union generals often copied Napoleon when having their pictures taken. The anonymous artist who created this print thought the pose suitable for this memorial portrait, combining it with the noted likeness of Lincoln.

Library of Congress

Columbia's noblest Sons

Following Lincoln's death, artists often created prints that linked George Washington, who was cast as the nation's founder, and Lincoln, portraying the martyred president as the savior of the Union. This example, published by Manson Long in New York in 1865, is typical. It depicts the figure of Columbia, the historic symbol of the United States, crowning the two heroes with laurel wreaths to honor their valiant deeds.

Next to Washington's portrait, important events of the American Revolution have been sketched: the Boston Tea Party, the signing of the Declaration of Independence, the surrender of the British at Yorktown. Lincoln's portrait is flanked by Civil War images: the bombardment of Fort Sumter, the battle between the *Monitor* and the *Merrimac,* and Lincoln's entry into Richmond at the war's end.

Beneath Columbia's firm right foot, the British lion slumbers peacefully. The American eagle emerges from behind her left foot. The guns of war, pointing out from beneath the portraits, have been silenced.

The Lincoln Museum

The Five-Dollar-Bill Portrait

This memorial card photograph also salutes the bond between Washington and Lincoln, "the Father and the Martyr." "They still live in our hearts," the card declares.
Museum of American Political Life/Steven Laschever

portrait of the president over its marquee, which bore the caption "We mourn the loss of an honest man." The Bowery Savings Bank also displayed a portrait of Lincoln and over it the words "Our Country Weeps."[2]

In such memorials the fallen president was often characterized as a martyr of liberty or the savior of the nation. The solemn and stately five-dollar-bill portrait was the one most frequently used to symbolize these qualities.

* * *

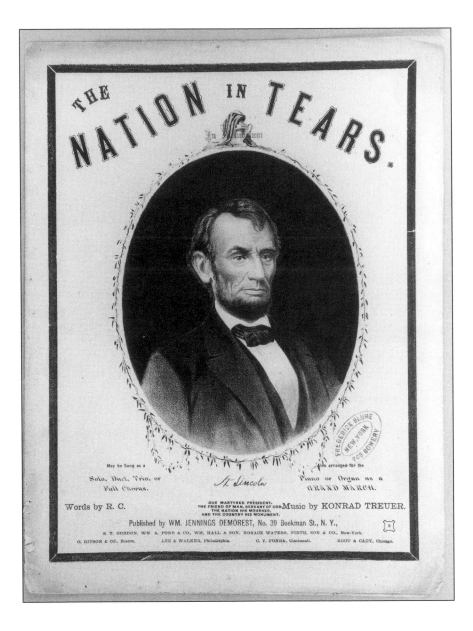

Lincoln's death prompted dozens of composers to create funeral marches and other pieces of commemorative music. Many of them were published as sheet music with elaborately decorated covers. "The Nation in Tears" is one example.

Museum of American Political Life/Steven Laschever

LINCOLN.

Henry Gugler, a German-born engraver, worked for three years to produce this exceptional engraving, which was published by William Pate & Co. in New York in 1869. Based on a painting by John H. Littlefield, who worked entirely from Berger's famous five-dollar-bill photograph, the print was generally known as the "Littlefield engraving." Senator Charles Sumner said, "Our martyred President lives in this engraving."

The Lincoln Museum

When Mathew Brady and Anthony Berger first looked at the photograph upon which the engravings in this chapter are based, and at the other photographs that were taken at the Brady studio that February afternoon in 1864, they surely had no idea what they had actually created. They could not have realized the countless different ways in which the images were to be used or the enormous impact they would have. But it is thanks to these images and the others presented in this book—and the prints, painted portraits, and sculpted likenesses derived from them—that the face of Lincoln is better known to Americans today than it was in his lifetime.

Notes

Picturing Lincoln

1. Lloyd Ostendorf, *Lincoln in Photographs: A Complete Album* (Dayton, Oh.: Rockywood Press, 1998), preface.

Chapter 1: The Tousled-Hair Photograph

1. David Herbert Donald, *Lincoln* (New York: Touchstone/Simon & Schuster, 1995), p. 196.
2. Ostendorf, p. 7.
3. Ibid.
4. Ibid.
5. Ibid.
6. Donald, p. 207.
7. Ostendorf, p. 47.

Chapter 2: At Cooper Union

1. James D. Horan, *Mathew Brady, Historian with a Camera* (New York: Crown, 1955), p. 31.
2. Ostendorf, p. 36.
3. Donald, p. 241.
4. Earl Schenck Miers (ed.), *Lincoln Day by Day: A Chronology, 1809–1865* (Washington: Lincoln Sesquicentennial Commission, 1960), vol. 2, p. 283.
5. Gabor S. Boritt, *The Historian's Lincoln* (Urbana, Ill.: University of Illinois Press, 1988), p. 34.
6. Horan, p. 35.
7. Horan, p. 32.

Chapter 3: The Penny Profile

1. Francis B. Carpenter, *Six Months at the White House with Abraham Lincoln: The Story of a Picture* (New York: Hurd & Houghton, 1866), p. 36.
2. Ibid.
3. Stephen B. Oates, *With Malice Toward None: A Life of Abraham Lincoln* (New York: HarperCollins, 1994), p. 380.

Chapter 4: Lincoln and Tad

1. Philip B. Kunhardt Jr., Philip Kunhardt III, and Peter W. Kunhardt, *Lincoln: An Illustrated Biography* (New York: Alfred A. Knopf, 1992), p. 394.

Chapter 5: The Five-Dollar-Bill Portrait

1. Ostendorf, p. 176.
2. Harold Holzer, Gabor S. Boritt, and Mark E. Neely Jr., *The Lincoln Image: Abraham Lincoln and the Popular Print* (New York: Charles Scribner's Sons, 1984), p. 161.

Further Reading

Boritt, Gabor S., *The Historian's Lincoln* (Urbana, Ill.: University of Illinois Press, 1988).

Carlebach, Michael J., *The Origins of Photojournalism in America* (Washington: Smithsonian Institution, 1992).

Donald, David Herbert, *Lincoln* (New York: Touchstone/Simon & Schuster, 1995).

Freedman, Russell, *Lincoln: A Photobiography* (New York: Clarion Books, 1987).

Holzer, Harold, Gabor S. Boritt, and Mark E. Neely Jr., *The Lincoln Image: Abraham Lincoln and the Popular Print* (New York: Charles Scribner's Sons, 1984).

Horan, James D., *Mathew Brady, Historian with a Camera* (New York: Crown, 1955).

Kunhardt, Philip B. Jr., Philip Kunhardt III, and Peter W. Kunhardt, *Lincoln: An Illustrated Biography* (New York: Alfred A. Knopf, 1992).

Miers, Earl Schenck (ed.), *Lincoln Day by Day: A Chronology, 1809–1865* (Washington: Lincoln Sesquicentennial Commission, 1960).

Oates, Stephen B., *With Malice Toward None: A Life of Abraham Lincoln* (New York: HarperCollins, 1994).

Ostendorf, Lloyd, *Lincoln in Photographs: A Complete Album* (Dayton, Oh.: Rockywood Press, 1998).

Sullivan, Edmund B., and Roger Fischer, *American Political Ribbons and Ribbon Badges* (Lincoln, Mass.: Quarterman Publishing, 1985).

Sullivan, George, *In Their Own Words: Abraham Lincoln* (New York: Scholastic Books, 2000).

Index

Page numbers in *italic* type refer to illustrations and/or captions.